# The Message

## Of The

# New Testament

Dr. John Thomas Wylie

**author**HOUSE®

*AuthorHouse™*
*1663 Liberty Drive*
*Bloomington, IN 47403*
*www.authorhouse.com*
*Phone: 1 (800) 839-8640*

*Published by AuthorHouse  05/26/2020*

*ISBN: 978-1-7283-6277-9 (sc)*
*ISBN: 978-1-7283-6276-2 (e)*

*The Apostolic Preaching And Its Developments (1944), (new edition) London, Eng.: Hodder & Stoughton, LTD*

*Morton, E. S. (1929) The Place Of Morality In The Thought Of Paul. Chester, PA.: (Publisher UNK)*

*Primitive Christianity In Its Contemporary Setting (1956) New York, NY.: Living Age Books, Meridan Books*

*The Ethics Of Paul (1957) Nashville, TN.: Abingdon Press, Apex Books.*

*Scripture taken from the King James Version of the Bible.*

*Scripture quotations marked NIV are taken from the Holy Bible, New International Version®. NIV®. Copyright © 1973, 1978, 1984 by International Bible Society. Used by permission of Zondervan. All rights reserved. [Biblica]*

*The Holy Bible (1978) New York, NY.: New York International Bible Society (Used By Permission)*

*Scripture quotations marked RSV are taken from the Revised Standard Version of the Bible, copyright © 1946, 1952, 1971 by the Division of Christian Education of the National Council of the Churches of Christ in the USA. Used by permission.*

*The Holy Bible (1901) The American Standard Version. Nashville, TN.: Thomas Nelson (Used By Permission)*

*The Holy Bible (1959) The Berkeley Version. Grand Rapids, MI.: Zondervan (Used By Permission)*

*Scripture quotations marked NASB are taken from the New American Standard Bible®, Copyright © 1960, 1962, 1963, 1968, 1971, 1972, 1973, 1975, 1977, 1995 by The Lockman Foundation. Used by permission.*

*Scripture quotations marked NLT are taken from the Holy Bible, New Living Translation, copyright © 1996, 2004, 2007. Used by permission of Tyndale House Publishers, Inc. Carol Stream, Illinois 60188. All rights reserved. Website*

*The New Testament In The Language Of The People (1937, 1949) Chicago, Ill.: Charles B. Williams, Bruce Humphries, Inc, The Moody Bible Institute (Used By Permission)*

*The New Testament In Modern English (1958) New York, NY.: J. B. Phillips, Macmillan (Used By Permission)*

*The Wycliff Bible Commentary (1962, 1968) Nashville, TN.: Chicago, Ill.: The Southwestern Company, The Moody Bible Institute Of Chicago*

# Contents

# Introduction

THE MESSAGE OF THE New Testament isn't the going ahead of new thoughts, nor ideas regarding God. It recounts a new and climactic act of God in sending Jesus Christ, and in shaping the Christian community as his own people, the true Israel. Some parts of the New Testament are proclamation of the good news concerning what God has done in Jesus Christ for the saving of humanity, and is intended to convert lost sinners to Christian believers.

Other parts are teaching or instruction, intended to built up the faith and life of believers with the goal that they might be mature Christians. Proclamation and teaching can't generally be unmistakably isolated, however it is well to remember that it contain both.

We will discuss the message of Jesus first, then the earliest Christian proclamation, next Paul's message, and the perspective of John. At long last we will summarize the unifying elements in the New Testament message.

# Chapter One

## Jesus And the Kingdom of God

"THE TIME IS FULFILLED, and the kingdom of God is at hand; repent, and believe in the gospel." These were the words with which Jesus began his career of preaching the gospel of God (Mark 1:15 RSV). The message of John the Baptist was fundamentally the same as:" "Repent, for the kingdom of heaven is at hand" (Matthew 3:2 RSV).

John had called upon men to repent and prepare themselves for the coming judgment, had baptized through water his followers, and had brought explicit gatherings of individuals to "bear fruit that befits repentance" (Matthew 3:8).

The entirety of the Gospels, with the exception of John, make Jesus' proclamation of the coming of the kingdom of God and his teachings about it central to his ministry. What did he mean by the kingdom of God? What did he think men should do in order to be prepared to enter it? What was his own relationship to the coming of the kingdom?" All these are crucial inquiries in the message of Jesus.

When Jesus used the expression "kingdom of God," he was not discussing a region, a country, or any real estate parcel. It would be considerably more exact for us to talk about the majesty, the kingship, or reign, or sovereignty of God. Besides, the expression "kingdom of heaven," used uniquely in Matthew, is a precise proportionate. It doesn't mean the kingdom in heaven; "heaven" is utilized as an equivalent word (a synonym) for God. At this time the Jews were here and there hesitant or reluctant to use the word "God" and fill in for it certain equivalent words or circumlocutions, of which "heaven" was a common one.

Jesus never plainly characterizes what he implies by the kingdom of God, however the phrase would have been recognizable to his listeners. The idea, however not the specific expression, returns to the Old Testament, and the expression itself was used by the Jews in their petitions, and on other occasion in the first century.

As far back as the times of Gideon the judge, the Israelites attempted to get him to serve as king over them and build up a ruling dynasty, however Gideon answered: "I won't rule over you, and my

Dr. John Thomas Wylie

son won't rule over you; the LORD will rule over you" (Judges 8:23 ASV).

When the monarchy of Saul was established, there were some who deciphered this as a rejection of Yahweh as King over Israel (I Samuel 8:7). Since the history of Israel, the overall conviction was that Yahweh was the True King of Israel; the king on the regal position of royalty (on the throne) was anointed to be God's representative and agent on earth.

In ancient Israel, nonetheless, there were two perspectives to the kingship of God; (1) from one perspective, they trusted God was the everlasting or eternal King of Israel, the Creator of the world and its Ruler; and yet, (2) they understood that God was not in fact King since his sovereignty was not recognized and his will was not obeyed - neither all through the entirety of Israel, nor among the countries of the world. Second Isaiah could prophesy of the time of when every knee would bow to Yahweh as God and King (Isaiah 45:23). In this manner one might say: God is King, and he is not yet King, for his sovereignty of God was a hope for the future.

In late Old Testament times and in the inter-testamental literature, an idea developed in apocalyptic thought which was to be significant for the conception of the kingdom of God. A dualism emerged which made a significant differentiation between the present age and the age-to-come.

Many Jews came to believe that the present age is under the rule of Satan, Beelzebub, or other evil powers (see Luke 4:6; 11:20; John 12:31; 14:30; 16:11; the thought is found in the Pseudepigrapha and the Dead Sea Scrolls). In this manner, the dominion of Satan must be broken before the ushering in of the age-to-come and the appearance of the kingdom of God.

Some of the teachings of Jesus speak about the kingdom of God as future. One of the most clear is Mark 9:1 RSV: "Truly, I say to you, there are some standing here who will not taste death before they see the kingdom of God with power." He taught his disciples to pray, "Thy kingdom come" (Matthew 6:10 RSV).

Jesus spoke of a future judgment where a separation would be made between the sheep and the goats, the righteous and the wicked, and to the former the King would say, "Come, O blessed of my Father, inherit the kingdom prepared for you from the foundation of the world" (Matthew 25:34 RSV).

At the Last Supper, Jesus said with respect to the cup, "I shall not drink again of the vine until that day when I drink it new it new in the kingdom of God" (Mark 14:25 RSV). In these, as well as other passages, Jesus seems to visualize a future coming of God's Kingdom.

Then again, some of Jesus teachings unmistakably stable as though he believed the kingdom had already come and was at that point present. While clarifying the importance of his expulsion of evil spirits (demons) (his exorcism), he says, "If it is by the Spirit of God that I cast out demons, the kingdom of God has come upon you" (Matthew 12:28 RSV; in Luke 11:20 the articulation "finger of God" is used rather than "Spirit of God").

Jesus interprets the casting out of demons as proof of the breaking of the power of Satan, so that the kingdom of God may come, and speaks about it as of now in some way present.

Another significant passage is Luke 17:20, 21 RSV. The Pharisees ask when the kingdom of God is coming, and Jesus answers that the kingdom doesn't accompany signs that can be watched, thus individuals won't state "Lo, here it is!" or "There it is." "For Behold," says Jesus, "the kingdom of God is in the midst you."

The expression can be rendered "within you," and a few researchers have deciphered this as implying that the kingdom is something completely spiritual, within the hearts of the believers. It is almost certain, be that as it may, taking into account the entry in general, that Jesus is truly saying that the kingdom of God is already in your midst.

In Matthew 11:11-14 and Luke 16:16 Jesus makes a distinction between the time of the law and the prophets which kept going to the time of John the Baptist, and the kingdom of God which-as he says-people are currently entering. Other teachings of Jesus, particularly a portion of his stories (parables), can be cited to as proof for his conviction that the kingdom of God was present in his own time.

How might we accommodate these two ideas that have all the earmarks of being very unique? Did Jesus believe that the kingdom of God had come in his own time and through his ministry, or did he look for it in the future? Interpreters have depended on other gadgets to dispose of one set of teachings or the other, or to state that one set has a place with one time of Jesus' life and the other set to another period.

It is wise to hold the both sets of teachings, and try to see how they are related in Jesus teaching as a whole. Jesus believed that in his ministry, prominently in his casting out of devils (demons), he was destroying the power of evil and enabling God's rule to show (manifest) itself, but yet he predicted (foresaw) that the complete acknowledgment and sign of God's reign lay in the future.

In the person and the entire ministry and life of Jesus the kingdom of God is as of now present in principle, and men may enter it by giving to God their absolute obedience; however the full realization of the kingship of God, the consummation of his kingdom, lies in the future. His teachings show he thought it would be sooner rather than later (in the near future), so he could say, "The kingdom of God is at hand."

In his teachings about the kingdom of God, Jesus didn't show enthusiasm for setting exact dates and giving the details of its coming (see Mark 13:32). His points was to announce its coming, and to call men to be set up to enter it or receive it. However, in his own vocation another time had opened up, and the powers of the age-to-come had already begun to be realized. God had already begun to rule in the earth in a more complete sense than he had ever done previously.

In this manner, the kingdom of God in Jesus' teaching isn't something that men are called upon to build on earth; nor is it something that bit by bit develops on earth. Above all it is God's kingdom, where "His Will" is done and which comes in his own way. However, men may prepare themselves to enter it and receive it by repentance, and by doing what John the Baptist called "bear fruit that befits repentance."

Many of Jesus' teachings talk about the lifestyle (way of life) of the individuals who are believers of the kingdom of God. Quite a bit of his teachinging in such manner is summarized in the Sermon on the Mount (Matthew 5-7). This message doesn't present the conditions one must meet so as to enter the kingdom of heaven for who could satisfy such conditions completely?

However, it describes the perfect lifestyle (way of life) for the individuals who are members of the kingdom of God. The first beatitude establishes the pace and declares the reason: "Blessed are the poor in spirit, for theirs is the kingdom of heaven."

Those who are in the kingdom are humble, meek, and merciful, pure in heart, prepared to endure persecution and affliction. They focus on a righteousness that surpasses that of the scribes and Pharisees, not nullifying the law but fulfilling its more deeper significance (meaning).

Murder comprises not just in the act of slaughtering (killing), but in the anger and hatred which inspire it. Adultery is not just an act of Infidelity, but, the lustful desire.

The disciple of the kingdom learns how to love his adversary just as his neighbor. In giving alms, in praying, and in fasting, he avoids public display and the longing to satisfy or please men, but looks to please God. He is single-hearted in his devotion to God, realizing that the can't serve God and Mammon at the same time.

Jesus holds up before his disciples as the goal of their way of life the imitation of God, the summons to "be perfect, as your heavenly Father is perfect" (5:48). This doesn't mean sinlessness, but rather unbiasedness (impartiality) and integrity, for example, God appears in making the sun arise on the evil and on the good, and sending rain on the just and the unjust.

Repentance and groundwork for the kingdom of God implied, in Jesus' teaching, radical and solid obedience to the will of God in a wide range of circumstances. Jewish educators some of the time discussed the need to take upon oneself the burden (yoke) of the kingdom of God, or the yoke of God's commands.

Along these lines, Jesus didn't teach that men could acquire the option to enter God's kingdom, for it was the gift of God, but that the individuals who were prepared for the kingdom of God must see that it meant discipline and obedience, as well as joy and fulfillment.

Jesus' emphasis was upon what men should be instead of what they should do, but what they were would unavoidably express in positive action, for a good tree must bring forth good fruit.

We may go now to the inquiry: what was Jesus' own relationship to the coming of the kingdom of God? Did he believe himself to be just a prophet, proclaiming the coming to the kingdom and showing men how to prepare themselves for it? Or on the other hand, would he say he was the Messiah with an extremely unique relationship to the kingdom? If he considered himself to be the Messiah, in what sense did he translate messiahship?

The responses to these inquiries are generally varied. A few researchers (scholars) of remarkable notoriety keep up that we can't generally know anything about Jesus' self-consciousness, about how he thought of himself. They state we can know only what the writers of the Gospels and the other New Testament books thought and believed about him. All were composed after the resurrection of Jesus, and everyone in the Christian community believed that Jesus was the Messiah, though they may have had various ways for expressing and explaining it.

We must admit it is incredibly hard for anybody to realize exactly what was Jesus' own conception of his mission, the way that the entirety of the New Testament was written after the resurrection should rule out all dogmatism in discussing this inquiry.

The earliest Christians believed, after the restoration of Jesus, that he was the Christ, the Son of God, one who had a one of a kind relationship (a unique relationship) to God and to the coming of his kingdom. Peter said at the finish of his message on Pentecost:

"Let all the house of Israel therefore know assuredly that God has made him both Lord and Christ, this Jesus whom you crucified" (Acts 2:36 RSV). The Christian church used numerous titles to communicate (express) its belief in the unique role of Jesus-Christ, Son of God, Son of Man, Son of David, Lord, Savior, Servant, Logos (Word), and numerous others.

Our statement "Christ" is the Greek Christos, which translated the Hebrew word Mashiah, "the anointed one." Sometimes Christ (or the Christ) is used in the Gospels in the sense of the Messiah, as in Mark 12:35; 13:21; John 1:20, 25; 3:28, and so forth...

Nonetheless, it soon became, after the resurrection, a proper name for Jesus, so that he could be called Christ, Jesus Christ, Christ Jesus, Our Lord Jesus Christ, and such. These happen particularly in Acts and the epistles. It is doubtful that Jesus at any point alluded to himself straightforwardly, in the soonest sources, as Messiah or Christ.

There is one truth of which we can be sure: Jesus didn't fulfill any of the typical Jewish

Dr. John Thomas Wylie

expectations concerning the Messiah. There was no orthodox, generally accepted doctrine of the Messiah, however Jesus didn't fit any of the types of Messiah that the Jews sought after. He was not a king situated upon an illustrious position of authority (a royal throne), administering justice and righteousness; he recognized the need to "render to Caesar the things that are Caesar's" (Mark 12:17 RSV).

Jesus was not a warrior at the head of a great company of soldiers, prepared to lead a revolt against Rome. He purposely dismissed the impulse to oust the Roman government forcibly. He was not a supernatural, angelic being who had originated from heaven on billows of glory.

Jesus was a person living very much as other men did; a portion of the religious leaders thought he was too human when he connected with delinquents and the outsiders of society. No, Jesus was not the Messiah in any of the for the most part acknowledged faculties, and we ought not be astonished that most of the Jews didn't hail him as such.

In the Synoptic Gospels Jesus doesn't say much regarding his own role, and talks moderately minimal about himself. In this regard the Gospel of John is extraordinary, for there he talks regularly of himself. In the prior Gospels, he needs to be known for what he does and for his teachings, not for the claims he makes for himself.

The story in Matthew 11:2-6 RSV is typical. When John heard in jail about the deeds of Jesus, he sent a portion of his disciples to ask, "Are you he who is come, or shall we search for another?" Jesus didn't straightforwardly answer their inquiry, but answered: "Go and tell John what you hear and see: the visually impaired get their sight and the faltering (lame) walk, lepers are cleansed and the hard of hearing (deaf) hear, and the dead are raised up, and the poor have good news preached to them. And blessed is he who takes no offense at me." Jesus' answer may be paraphrased: "Take a look at what I am doing, and from that make your own conclusion as to whether I am the expected Messiah."

The Gospel of Mark has a theory concerning the "messianic secret" of Jesus. Mark says that many demons and unclean spirits that Jesus cast out remembered him, however Jesus requested them not to uncover what his identity was (1:24, 34; 3:11, 12). Mark likewise says that Jesus advised the anecdote so as to mystify the people, yet showed their significance to his own followers (disciples) covertly (4:11, 12).

Following Peter's admission at Caesarea-Philippi, Mark says that Jesus "charged them to enlighten nobody regarding him" (8:30). Most interpreters believe that somewhat this theory of a messianic secret is Mark's method for clarifying why the hoards didn't recognize Jesus as the Messiah and accept him; absolutely his clarification concerning the anecdotes is at variance with Jesus' genuine reason (true purpose) in teaching through parables.

By the by, there might be behind Mark's theory the way that Jesus was hesitant to be viewed as the Messiah, for there were implications in that term that he didn't care for. He dismissed the nationalistic, political, and materialistic parts of the messianic desires that were abroad among the people.

Taking into account this, a few scholars believe that Jesus didn't profess to be the Messiah, nor wish to be considered all things considered. They believe he wished to be referred to as a teacher or rabbi, and a prophet. He announced the coming of a kingdom and of a Messiah, and he called upon his listeners to repent, as the Old Testament prophets did, but had no special relationship to that kingdom.

A portion of the expressions of Jesus give proof that he thought of himself as a prophet. At Nazareth he stated, "A prophet isn't without honor, except in his own country, and among his own kin, and in his own house" (Mark 6:4 RSV). He said that it was not fitting for a prophet to die away from Jerusalem (Luke 13:33).

Following the triumphal passage into Jerusalem, when the people asked, "Who is this?" the crowds answered:" 'This is the prophet Jesus from Nazareth of Galilee" (Matthew 21:11 RSV). Other passages could be referred to that show Jesus was considered as a prophet in his own time. To be a prophet, a representative for God like the prophets of the Old Testament, was a high calling and a difficult mission.

In any case, there are numerous things in the earliest traditions concerning Jesus and his life that make it difficult to accept that he wished to be viewed as only as a prophet, and that he made no claim to be the Messiah in any sense.

When Jesus was baptized by John, he heard a voice from heaven saying, "Thou art my beloved Son; with thee I am well pleased" (Mark 1:11

KJV). These words join two Old Testament verses, Psalm 2:7 and Isaiah 42:1. Peter confessed the conviction and belief of the disciples when he stated: "You are the Christ" (Mark 8:29 RSV). Jesus didn't dismiss this assignment, nor reprimand or rebuke Peter for his answer, however he accepted it with some reservation.

The narrative of the triumphal section of Jesus into Jerusalem toward the start of his last week has every appearance of being an arranged passage of a messianic figure, and he was hailed as such.

At the Last Supper, he offered the cup as representing to the blood of the covenant, and talked about anticipating drinking the cup in the kingdom of God. At the preliminary (trial) before the high priest, we read that Jesus was asked, "Are you the Christ, the Son of the Blessed?" and Jesus answered, "I am" (Mark 14:61, 62 RSV).

Notwithstanding these particular occurrences, we should see that Jesus brought men to follow him, to become his disciples. He called upon them to repent and prepare for the kingdom, but he likewise called upon them to renounce numerous material things and come after him. The number of the disciples who followed him in this way was much greater than the twelve apostles.

Jesus thus spoke with authority, and with an urgency for personal decision to follow him, that was more prominent than one would anticipate from a rabbi (teacher) or prophet.

It is no doubt, that Jesus considered himself as the Messiah, but not in the popular sense. He reinterpreted the idea of messiahship in a new and creative manner, providing for "Messiah" a new meaning. The clue of information to this reinterpretation is in his use of the irregular term, Son of man.

The term Son of man happens more frequently in the Gospels than some other messianic term, and it generally happens in the sayings of Jesus. It is used once in a while (rarely) outside the Gospels.

This term has three distinct implications. Now and then it is just another method for saying "mankind" or "a human being," as in Psalm 8:4. This is its significance in Mark 2:27 RSV: "The sabbath was made for man, not man for the sabbath; so the Son of man is lord even of the sabbath."

Another utilization of the title, Son of man, was to portray the supernatural, angelic figure that numerous Jews anticipated that the Messiah should be; they anticipated his coming on clouds of glory to bring deliverance and judgment. This use is based on Daniel 7, where we read that "one like a son of man" preceded the Ancient of Days and was given everlasting dominion, glory, and kingdom.

The Son of man in the Book of Enoch is explicitly a messianic figure. He is portrayed as coming to sit on the throne of glory and judge the nations; he is pre-existent; and he is "the anointed one" and "the light of the gentiles."

In many passages of the Gospels the Son of man is portrayed as coming in the future with the blessed messengers (angels), to sit on his glorious throne, judging the nations and saving the righteous. Some of these passages are Mark 8:38; 13:36; 14:62; Matthew 19:28; 25:31; Luke 18:8.

There is a third importance to the term, Son of man, that is completely new, and is interesting with Jesus. He discusses the suffering of the Son of man, and consolidates in his truisms about the Son of man a portion of the attributes of the Suffering Servant of the Lord delineated in Isaiah 53 and related passages of Second Isaiah.

Following Peter's confession, Mark says that

Jesus "began to teach them that the Son of man must suffer many things, and be rejected by the elders and the chief priests and the scribes, and be killed (be crucified), and following three days rise again" (Mark 8:31 RSV). Peter rebuked Jesus, for he was unable to comprehend this sort of messiahship. But, twice Jesus repeated these predictions of his coming suffering (Mark 9:31; 10:33). Concerning himself Jesus further said, "For the Son of man also came not to be served but to serve, and to give his life as a ransom for many" (Mark 10:45 RSV).

We close, at that point, that Jesus viewed himself as the Messiah, but accepted the designation with some hesitance (reluctance) and reinterpreted the idea it associated with a new, creative way. For his reinterpretation he chose the figure of the Son of man, presumably on the grounds that it was not related with political and nationalistic aspirations, and it could be associated with his suffering as a human being.

It was a to some degree a mysterious title, maybe impossible for Gentiles to comprehend. Jewish followers of Jesus had incredible trouble understanding that the Messiah must suffer; that is the reason they abandoned him at the hour of the torturous killing (the crucifixion).

The early Christian community joined the last two implications of the expression "Son of man": they thought of Jesus as the Son of man who had suffered, died, and risen once more, and they anticipated when he would return on clouds of glory with the heavenly angels as a triumphant Son of man. Did Jesus himself hold both of these implications, expecting to return in bodily form as a triumphant Messiah? This is an inquiry we can't answer, and it is smarter to say that we don't know whether he had such an expectation.

Following 1900 years he has not returned as such, but he has returned in spirit to many people and in his Church, the "body of Christ."

The significant inquiry we should pose concerning Jesus is this: did God truly send him, and-whatever designation he used or accepted - did God through him usher in the kingdom of God?: To this inquiry the Christian answers in faith: Yes!

# Chapter Two

## The Earliest Christian Preaching

NOT LONG AFTER THE resurrection of Jesus, his disciples had the experience of Pentecost; as Acts 2 relates it, they were filled with the Holy Spirit, and men from different nations heard them talking each in his own language. The witnesses achieved numerous signs and wonders.

The members from the Christian community appreciated an exceptionally close fellowship, expressed for a time in the common ownership of possessions. They continued to worship in the temple, and "breaking bread in their homes, they participated in nourishment with happy and liberal (generous) hearts, praising God and having favor with all the people" (Acts 2:46, 47 RSV).

The witnesses and others proclaimed Jesus as the Messiah, and additions were made to the church. Time and again a portion of the witnesses were captured by Jewish authorities, however, subsequently released. The first Christian martyr, Stephen, was executed by stoning. From that point onward, the Christians were aggrieved decisively, and a considerable lot of them were scattered all through Judea and Samaria to preach the good news of Jesus Christ.

Different articulations are used to show the nature of the early preaching; in the Synoptic Gospels and Acts we read of Jesus or the apostles "preaching the kingdom of God," while in the Pauline epistles the standard expression is "preaching Christ."

In an investigation of major significance, C. H. Dodd has tried to characterize the substance of this earliest Christian preaching, or apostolic preaching. He discovers its substance essentially in the five discourses of Peter recorded in Acts 2:14-40; 3:12-26; 4:8-12; 5:29-32; and 10:34-43, and the discourse of Paul at Pisidian Antioch given in Acts 13:16-41.

Also, he accepts that hints of it very well may be found in a portion of Paul's letters, such an I Corinthians 15:1-7, 23-28; Romans 1:1-4; 8:31-34; 10:8-9; Galatians 1:3, 4; and in Peter 1:10-12; 3:18-22.

This early Christian preaching was a proclamation of the good news of what God had done and would do in Christ for man's salvation.

It is regularly alluded to in present day takes a shot at the New Testament by its Greek name, Kerygma. In Greek this word could mean either the act of preaching or the content of what was preached.

It is in the last sense that the word is frequently used today, for all intents and purposes as a technical term. In many regards the word gospel, "the good news," is synonymous; truth be told, New Testament scholars themselves all the more frequently used the word gospel (evangelion) for the content of the earliest preaching than the word kerygma.

The contents of the kerygma, or the gospel as it was preached in its earliest form, was as per the following:

(1) The time of fulfillment of God's promises to Israel has now unfolded. The predictions of the Old Testament are currently happening (coming to pass). The individual items of the kerygma are typically upheld by quotations from the Old Testament, for example, passages of Joel 2, Psalms 2 and 110, Deuteronomy 18, Isaiah 53, and others.

(2) This fulfillment has taken place through

the ministry, the death, and the resurrection of Jesus Christ.

(a) He was conceived of the seed of David.

(b) In his ministry "God anointed Jesus of Nazareth with the Holy Spirit and with power... he went about doing good and healing all that were oppressed by the devil, for God was with him" (Acts 10:38 RSV). In such a way Jesus of Nazareth was "a man attested to you by God with mighty works and wonders and signs which God did through him" (2:22).

(c) But Jesus was put to death on the cross. This was done through the plan and foreknowledge of God, but at the hands of wicked men who denied the Holy and Righteous One.

(d) God raised up Jesus from the dead, loosing the aches of death, and made him Lord and Christ. Of his resurrection a considerable lot of the early disciples were witnesses.

(3) The risen Jesus has been lifted up to the right hand of God in heaven, as Prince and Savior, the messianic head of the new Israel.

(4) The presence of the Holy Spirit in the church is the sign of Christ's power and wonder. Consequently the Holy Spirit was poured out on the Church upon the arrival of Pentecost. Luke

frequently stresses the presence and the leading of the Spirit, thus additionally Paul in his letters.

(5) Christ will before long come back from heaven to perfect (consummate) the messianic age, and be judge of the living and the dead. The desire for the arrival of Christ was clear in the early long periods of the church; however it turned out to be less distinctive (vivid) as time went on, and the desire for the subsequent appearance was supplanted by different thoughts in certain compositions, it is found even in the most recent books of the New Testament.

(6) The kerygma closes with an appeal for repentance and belief in Christ, now and again for baptism for the sake of Jesus; and with the proposal of forgiveness of sins and the coming of the Holy Spirit. One of the most complete proclamations of this is in the expressions of Peter in Acts 2:39: "Repent, and be baptized every one of you in the name of Jesus Christ for the forgiveness of your sins; and you will receive the gift of the Holy Spirit." Those who acknowledged the appeal would experience the salvation promised to the members of the elect community, the true Israel.

The kerygma was addressed to the individuals who were not believers in Christ to convert them to the Christian faith. Its purpose was to proselytize (evangelize). Throughout time teaching was produced for the Christians, with the goal that they may become mature.

We need not assume that the entirety of the above components were remembered for each Christian message addressed to potential converts, nor that there was no variation from these components.

The above sums up in a helpful manner the total message as it was preached to convert Jews or Gentiles to faith in Jesus Christ.

The proclaiming is firmly identified with the message of Jesus, expanding it in the light of his entire profession. We have seen components: (1) The time is fulfilled; (2) the kingdom of God is at hand; therefore, (3) repent and believe in the gospel.

The kerygma follows the same outline, however gives the significance of the whole vocation (career) of Jesus-from birth to the second coming for the Christian believer.

The kerygma clearly didn't put incredible emphasis on the ministry of Jesus. As time went on, when the apostles and eyewitnesses of the ministry died, and the return of Jesus was delayed, the Gospels were composed. They follow as a rule the example of the kerygma, but fill in numerous details of the life and teaching of Jesus. They were proposed both for the conversion of believers and for the instruction of Christians in the content of their faith.

# Chapter Three

## The New Creation "in Christ" (Paul)

"I AM NOT ASHAMED of the gospel: it is the power of God for salvation to each one who has faith, to the Jew first and furthermore to the Greek. For in it the righteousness of God is revealed through faith; as it is stated, "He who through faith is righteous shall live" (Romans 1:16, 17 RSV). These two passages sum up a significant number of the trademark highlights (characteristics) of Paul's message.

His message was based upon the early kerygma we have sketched out. Despite the fact that Paul obviously didn't know Jesus in his earthly vocation, he must have know the earliest Christian message during the time he was mistreating, persecuting the Christians.

He doubtlessly more likely than not tuned in to the earliest Christian evangelists of the gospel; to him their claim that the crucified Christ was the Messiah, and that he had risen from the dead, more likely than not appeared to be blasphemy.

When he was converted making progress toward Damascus, Paul saw the risen Christ and, in a little while, he started to preach Christ.

Three years after his conversion he went to Jerusalem and went through a fortnight chatting with Peter and James the brother of Jesus (Galatians 1:18-20); and afterward fourteen years after the fact he was in Jerusalem, evidently at the hour of the Jerusalem Council, and consulted with the apostles once more.

This time he said that the leaders of the church, "those who were of repute," added nothing to his gospel (2:6). Recorded as a hard copy to the Corinthians, he spoke about "what I also received" (I Corinthians 15:3). Paul believed that he got his gospel by disclosure (Revelation); it was not man's gospel (Galatians 1:11). By and by, it depended on the earliest Christian preaching, going beyond it and interpreting it in the light of Paul's own experiences and contemplation.

Paul's religious philosophy (Paul's Theology) establishes his endeavor to clarify the significance of his converion, against the foundation of his prior training and involvement with Judaism, and in the light of his resulting life as a Christian missionary.

Paul's letters were addressed to people and churches that were at that point Christian; consequently they contain more that ought to be called teaching than appeals for conversion. Since Paul's message is contained for us in these letters, we can't hope to discover in them a system of doctrine.

Paul was a mind boggling character, in whom the man of action and the scholar were astoundingly consolidated. It was his inclination to see numerous things as far as absolute abstracts, of black or-white, that others didn't see so clearly contrasted. His message along these lines contains components that are incomprehensible, if not conflicting; it isn't unusual that II Peter 3:15, 16 says that "our beloved brother Paul" wrote in his letters "some things hard to understand."

Paul believed that all men are sinners, and remain needing salvage from the power of transgression (sin), and reconciliation to God. "All have sinned and fall short of the glory of God" (Romans 3:23 RSV). For Paul, sin was not only an act or a series of acts; it was a state or condition in which men live, a fundamental wrongness in all men.

It is the exceptionally the opposite of faith:

"whatever doesn't proceed from faith is sin" (Romans 14:23 RSV). He doesn't say much regarding the origin of sin. Some of the time he says that sin began with Adam, the predecessor of humankind, the ancestor of the human race, or the representative, typical man (Romans 5:12-14). At other times he seems to believe that sin originates with "elemental spirits," the satanic forces or demonic powers of the universe that are at war with man and God.

Man living in sin lives according to "the flesh." This doesn't mean for Paul that the material side of man's nature is in itself sinful, as appeared differently in relation to the spiritual side, or the soul. "Flesh" some of the time signifies man's lower nature, yet for the most part it is man's whole nature separated from and contrary to God. Living as indicated by the flesh is something contrary to life in the Spirit, the life of faith.

Man along these lines remains needing salvage, rescue from sin, and God in his love has given the way for rescue. "God shows his love for us in that while we were yet sinners Christ died for us...sending his own Son in the likeness of sinful flesh and for sin, he condemned sin in the flesh" (Romans 5:8; 8:3 RSV). Christ, sent by a loving Father to the world, is his solution to man's need of rescue from slavery to sin.

Man, on his part, is saved from the power of transgression (sin) by faith. This, obviously, is a focal word for Paul. Paul himself had attempted to find salvation from transgression and fellowship with God through keeping of the Law, however he failed. Romans 7:7-25 is a portrayal of how Paul in his pre-Christian days looked to find harmony (peace) with God by the keeping of the Law, but couldn't do as such; it is additionally a depiction of run of the mill man looking for salvation thusly.

He says, "I delight in the law of God, in my deepest self, however I find in my members another law at war with the law of my mind and making me hostage (captive) to the law of sin which dwells in my members. Wretched man that I am! Who will deliver me from this body of death?" Paul's own answer is: "Thanks be to God through Jesus Christ our Lord!" (Romans 7:22-25 RSV).

By faith Paul didn't mean essentially a conclusion or opinion about Christ, not a assent to a lot of doctrines about him. He implied trust in the living Christ, trust in the faithfulness of God.

In the fullest sense, faith is man's wholehearted acceptance of the good news that the saving grace of God has been freely offered to him in Christ. It is the precondition for receiving God's salvation, but it involves the nonstop requirement for submission to God and obedience to him (Romans 1:5).

Faith is the response of man to the revelation of God in Christ, "For by grace you have been saved through faith; and this isn't your own doing, it is the gift of God-not due to works, least any man should boast" (Ephesians 2:8, 9 RSV). Faith implies the relinquishment of all reliance upon one's self and one's own legitimacy, one's own merit and complete dependence upon the grace of God, as revealed above all else in Jesus Christ.

The Christ of whom Paul frequently speaks is the crucified and risen Christ, the living Lord. He says little regarding the life and teachings of Jesus before the torturous killing (crucifixion), in spite of the fact that he had faith in the full humanity of Christ and he more likely than not expected that his readers knew about the earthly profession and teaching of Jesus. For Paul the cross and the resurrection were of central importance.

The titles and names which Paul utilizes for

Jesus are revealing. He uses the name Jesus alone for the earthly man. Christ, the equivalent of the Messiah, has become for him for all intents and purposes a part of the name, instead of a title, with the goal that he can talk about Jesus Christ or Christ Jesus, or just Christ. He doesn't use the title Son of man, which would have been useless to Hellenistic readers of his letters.

He speaks about Jesus as conceived of the seed of David, but doesn't call him Son of David, potentially in light of the fact that it would have appeared to be excessively nationalistic. His preferred title is Lord (kyrios). This title likely didn't start with Paul, for it is found in the Aramaic expression which was most likely used in the Palestinian churches, Marana tha, signifying "Our Lord, come!" (I Corinthians 16:22). Lord is a title which would have been promptly comprehended in the Hellenistic world as the head of a religious cult. Since it is used in the Old Testament of God (a similar word kyrios in the Septuagint), it is here and there hard to decide if Paul is speaking of God or of Christ.

Paul regularly calls Christ "Son of God.' He says that he was "designated Son of God in power as per the Spirit of holiness by his resurrection from the dead" (Romans 1:4).

There are barely any passages in which Paul may call Christ "God," especially Romans 9:5 and II Thessalonians 1:12. In these passages the translation isn't sure, and they may allude to God separate from Christ. In Colossians 1:19; 2:9 he says that the "fulness of God" dwelt in Christ.

However, Paul in various places makes an understood partition among God and Christ, and keeps up his strict Jewish monotheism. For instance, in I Corinthians 8:6 RSV he says, "for us there is one God, the Father, from whom are all things and for whom we exist, and one Lord, Jesus Christ, through whom we are all things and through whom we exist."

It is maybe astounding to most readers to find that Paul uses the term Savior of Christ only once, Philippians 3:20 (cf. Ephesians 5:23). This term appears frequently in the pastoral Epistles and II Peter, later than Paul.

Paul uses various terms to communicate what God through Christ, especially in his death and resurrection, does for the man of faith: redemption, justification, reconciliation, adoption, victory over satanic or demonic powers, sacrifice, forgiveness, and new creation. A large portion of these terms are to be considered as synonymous; they are varying attempts on Paul's part to clarify what God in Christ has done for him, and can do for any believer. It is difficult to place into precise words.

Paul knew that in his conversion he had encountered an enormous upheaval (revolution) in his life. He was overwhelmed by the fact that, even while he was a sinner, Christ died for him and carried him into fellowship with God. In Christ, Paul found discharge from his internal disturbance, freedom from the Law, and a life of joy of and peace. It was difficult to articulate (to put into words) what Christ could accomplish for the man of faith, and Paul attempted a several unique ways. This figures are drawn from different everyday areas of life -the law court, the marketplace center, the cult, the battlefield, etc.

Like a slave ransomed from his master, the believer is redeemed from slavery to sin. As an accused man standing before a bar for equity (justice) might be absolved and announced guiltless, the believer is "justified" by God, he is acquitted, and set in a right relationship with his accuser. Salvation means reconciliation among

God and man, who had been estranged before: "God in Christ reconciling the world to himself" (II Corinthians 5:19 RSV). The believer is not, at this point a slave, but is adopted as a son by God, and as an heir of God, he is a fellow heir with Christ (Romans 8:17; Galatians 4:5-7).

The work of Christ meant not just that he vanquished sin for the individual, but also won the victory over the "elemental spirits," the devilish powers (demonic powers) of the universe that lead man into sin. In Colossians 2:15 a distinctive analogy is utilized: God "disarmed the principalities and powers and made a public example of them, triumphing over them" in the cross of Christ. The salvation secured by Christ is a cosmic salvation, saving the entire universe from the power of sin and death.

Sometimes the death of Christ is depicted as a sacrifice. This isn't as prominent in Paul's letters as in some other parts of the New Testament (as, in Hebrews), however it is available in passages, for example, Romans 3:25; 5:9 and others. As a sacrifice, the death of Christ served to set man in a favorable relationship with God.

Paul strangely makes little use of the conception of forgiveness of sins, and the related appeal for repentance. Forgiveness of sin is referenced distinctly in Colossians 1:14 and Ephesians 1:7. Most likely forgiveness of sins is inferred in some of Paul's different representations. Perhaps the explanation he speaks so little of forgiveness of sins is that he was concerned not so much with the forgiveness of sins is implied in some of Paul's other metaphors.

In these representations for crafted by Christ, Paul is endeavoring to state that man is conveyed from his servitude to sin and his offense from God, and is set in the right relationship with God, a relationship of fellowship and love, best communicated by the figure of the Son who can call out to God, "Abba! Father!" (Romans 8:15; Galatians 4:6).

The man who in faith accepts what God has done for him in Christ becomes a new creature, a new man. He puts on a new nature, and has put off his old nature. "If any one is in Christ, he is a new creature" (II Corinthians 5:17).

Paul clarifies what occurs as such. When the pre-existing Christ came to earth and became a man, he took upon himself a full humankind, identifying himself completely with the entirety of humanity. He carried on with a completely human life, being tempted to sin but not sinning. His life was to be indeed more completely human than any that has been lived, for he lived as God desires man to live; he was completely submissive, fully obedient to God, even to death on the cross. In the cross the love of God and the evil (wickedness) of man were both completely, fully revealed, and God's love vanquished (conquered) man's sin.

The man who has faith identifies himself with Christ; he accepts what God has done, and he becomes a new man "in Christ." As Christ had identified himself with sinful mankind, so the believer identifies himself with the perfect Christ. Accordingly, he becomes a new creature, a new man "in Christ."

Paul put incredible emphasis on the solidarity of humanity. Similarly as he could state that in Adam all sin, so he can say that in Christ all have the possibility through faith of a new life (Romans 5:12-21).

For Paul, the symbol for the death of the old nature and formation of the new nature was the ceremony of baptism. "Do you not realize that we all who have been baptized into Christ Jesus were baptized into his death? We were buried accordingly with him by baptism into his death, so that as Christ was raised from the dead by the glory of the Father, we also may walk in newness of life" (Romans 6:3, 4 RSV; see likewise Colossians 2:12).

In Galatians 3:27 RSV, he says: "As many of you as were baptized into Christ have put on Christ." Baptism was the sign and seal of man's death to an old nature and resurrection to a new; it was likewise the act of initiation into the church which, as we will see, Paul called "the body of Christ."

The life of the Christian was for Paul a life "in Christ." This is one of the most characteristic and regular expressions of Paul. He uses the expression or phrase "in Christ" or "in the Lord" multiple times; a couple of times he uses the comparative expression "in the Spirit," clearly with the equivalent or fundamentally the same as importance. Paul some of the time speaks of Christ as being "in you," or in the believer, but not so regularly as he speaks about the believer being in Christ.

The believer who is "in Christ" has the all of the benefits of salvation - peace, joy, freedom, power to carry on with a life of love for God and of his fellow men, and numerous others.

Paul's perspective on the Christian life has been called by certain interpreters Christ-mysticism. This is proper, if we see unmistakably what Paul didn't mean, and what sort of mysticism it was. It was not the kind of mysticism in which man could become totally caught up (completely absorbed) in the divine, in God or Christ. Paul was constantly aware of the way that God remains God and man remains man; they can't become one. Man looks for fellowship with God, not absorption in the divine.

Moreover, Paul didn't have in mind an estatic mysticism, however he himself was capable of estatic mysticism (see his conversion, and II Corinthians 12:1-5). It was ethical mysticism, in which the believer looks to carry on with an actual life deserving of, or worthy of the Christ with whom he has union.

Paul's perspective on Christian life as a new life "in Christ" drives us to a conversation of his attitude toward the Law and toward moral standards in general. His perspective is in no way, shape or form simple to grasp, and involves paradoxes.

Paul had sought as a Pharisaic Jew to keep the Law and therefore to be justified in the sight of God, yet he felt ceaselessly frustrated in his effort. He couldn't wholly keep the Law, and he found no obvious peace. Peace came to him only through faith in Christ. Accordingly, Paul regularly expressed unquestionably that no man can be justified, saved, or reconciled to God by keeping the Law, or by doing benevolent acts (good works).

By the Law, Paul for the most part implied the legal part of the Old Testament, or the Old Testament as a whole; yet he perceived that even the Gentiles have an concept of natural law, and of conscience (Romans 2:13-16). Abraham, the ancestor of the Hebrews, was saved by his faith, not by the Law, which came after his time (Romans 4).

For Paul "Christ is the end of the law, that every one who has faith may be justified" (Romans 10:4 RSV). The Christian is dead to the Law. Nevertheless, Paul could say: "The law is holy, and the commandment is holy and just and good" (Romans 7:12 RSV). The Jewish law had value in that it told man what sin is, stirred his conscience, and lead him to Christ.

The Christian, at that point, isn't entirely excluded from law as a principle of life: Paul can discuss fulfilling the "law of Christ" (Galatians 6:2), and state, "he who loves his neighbor has fulfilled the law. The commandments...are summarized in this sentence, "You shall love your neighbor as yourself" (Romans 13:8, 9 RSV).

Paul never does really distinguish in his letters between the moral law and the ceremonial law, however he suggests that the Christian should fulfill the moral law of the Old Testament, and he himself (as one who had been brought into the world a Jew) did on some occasions keep regulations of the ceremonial law.

The logical way of expressing Paul's position is to state that the man of faith, who is a new creature in Christ, will do what he ought to do because he now wants to do it.

He does from inward desire what the man under the Law did from outer compulsion. His life naturally produces the fruit of the Spirit, and his faith works through love(Galatians 5:6). Paul himself could state:

I through the law died to the law, that I mighyt live to God. I have been crucified with Christ; it is no longer I who live, but Christ who lives in me; and the life I now live in the flesh I live by faith in the Son of God, who loved me and gave himself for me (Galatians 2:19, 20).

This is the true Christ-mysticism of Paul.

With this perspective on the Christian's freedom from law and his new life "in Christ," Paul should logically not have needed to offer ethical advice to his readers. Yet, in reality he does just that as it were to a great extent. His letters frequently contain an enormous section dealing with practical issues that give specific moral directives or counsels, at times with advice on special problems on which he was consulted.

One purpose behind this is Paul's message was broadly misunderstood, particularly among the Gentiles who didn't have the high moral standards of the Jews. Some thought he implied the Christian is liberated from all law and can do whatever he likes to do; they confused freedom for license. Another explanation is that there is in Paul's message (and frequently in the Christian message in any form) an ultimate paradox: the Christian must be admonished to strive, with the assistance of God, to become that which he already is by the grace of God.

Paul frequently exhorts his readers to strive,

with the help of God, commendably of their calling, to live as indicated by the new nature that they have put on, and the like. The paradox is most clearly expressed in Philippians 2:12, 13 RSV: "Work out your own salvation with fear and trembling; for God is at work in you, both to will and to work for his good pleasure."

With respect to ethical inspiration (motivation), Paul sometimes spoke to the words or the example of Jesus, particularly his humility and meekness. Some of the time he even reproved others to follow his own model. Be that as it may, his appeal most importantly was for Christians to live worthily of their union with Christ; this union was to be both their motive and their dynamic for living.

Paul's ethics depend to a great extent upon the Old Testament and emerge out of his Jewish foundation, however at some points he may have been influenced by Hellenistic ethical ideals of the times, especially of the Stoics. Morton S. Enslin summaries four essential statutes of Paul and are as follows:

(1) "Separate yourselves from all that would defile." Paul cautions particularly against sexual

laxity of the sort which was across the board in the Roman world among non-Jews.

(2) "Be steadfast in all conduct of life." "Stand firm" is a most loved directive; the Christian is to persevere, be courageous, be willing to suffer affliction. Paul says the slave ought to obey his master, and the master be reasonable (fair) and just toward his slave; the church member ought to obey those set above him; the Christian should respect Roman authorities.

(3) "Through love serve each other." Here Paul uncovers close kinship to the teaching of Jesus.

(4) "Rejoice in the Lord always; again I will say, rejoice." These expressions of Paul, written in prison (Philippians 4:4 RSV), may sound abnormal as a ethical statute, but they normal for him. He understood how evil this world is, yet he accepted that Christ had overcome the world and the Christian should rejoice in view of his hope for the future.

Paul didn't think about his believers as being saved merely as people, and didn't anticipate that the Christian should live a solitary life. He set up churches in numerous parts of the world, and had consistent tension (anxiety) and care for them. He considered the Christian To be as a member of the church, of the community of the new covenant, the true Israel.

Paul's most characteristic term for the church is "the body of Christ." In I Corinthians 12:12-30 and Romans 12:4-8 he uses the figure to underscore the assortment of gifts inside the church, the shared reliance of the members (mutual dependence), and the full importance of all the members. In Colossians 1:18 and Ephesians 1:23; 4:16; 5:23, the figure is used to stress the unity of the church and the headship of Christ.

Paul may have used the expression "body of Christ" in an exceptionally reasonable sense: the church is the material and earthly body of the spiritual Christ who is exalted to heaven. In other passages, the church is the sanctuary (the temple) where God dwells (I Corinthians 3:16; II Corinthians 6:16; Ephesians 2:19-22), the bride of Christ (Ephesians 5:23-32), or the "Israel of God" (Galatians 6:16).

Individual members of the churches were to Paul "saints" or "brethren." The previous term was not used in light of the fact that all Christians were viewed as perfect and upright in their lives. "Saint" doesn't suggest godliness, but instead a specific relationship to God. Paul tended to the church of Corinth as follows:

"To the church of God which is at Corinth, to those sanctified in Christ Jesus, called to be saints..." It is superbly obvious and clear from I Corinthians that there were members of the church in Corinth who were a long way from saintly in the ethical sense; the letter uncovers both serious party division and extra-marital perversion of an unspeakable kind (5:1).

The individuals who were in the church were "saints" since they had surrendered themselves to God through faith in Christ, and had been set apart by God and called to a new life.

Paul believed in the second coming to Christ. This conviction (this belief) shows up all through his letters, but the hope for the second coming is more distinctive in the early letters than in later ones. His earliest letters, I and II Thessalonians, were composed to manage issues of the second coming.

In the first of these Paul appears to look for the advent of Christ sooner rather than later (in the near future). In later letters, the expectation (hope) isn't deserted, yet the accentuation come to be put more upon the life of the believer "in Christ" from day to day.

Paul never indulged in apocalyptic catastrophic theories of a detailed sort, and his letters are far unique in relation to the Book of Revelation. One specific teaching of Paul's was affected by his faith in the return of Christ. In answer to an inquiry from Corinth with respect to marriage of the individuals who were single, Paul advised them to cease from marriage "taking into account the impending distress" and on the grounds that "the appointed time has grown very short" (I Corinthians 7:25-35 RSV).

Paul never surrendered belief in the second coming of Christ, and the coming of a day of judgment, as a time when God would punish insidious and the individuals who had received Christ would see the consummation of their salvation. He continually appealed to his readers to live in in such a way to be prepared for the return of the Lord, for he may come at an unforeseen time "like a thief in the night."

Dr. John Thomas Wylie

# Chapter Four

## Eternal Life (John)

THE GOSPEL OF JOHN stands apart from the Synoptic Gospels, as we found in the last chapter. It is the most recent of the four, and follows to some degree distinctive authentic structure; it has a tone that is not the same as the others. It appears to be likely that the Gospel and the three Epistles of John (but not Revelation) were composed by a same man-John the Elder, who lived and wrote in Ephesus close to the end of the first century A.D.

The extraordinary distinction between his Gospel and the others is that his is substantially more a theological understanding (interpretation) of the life of Jesus than they are. None of the Gospels is an entirely objective, clear history of Jesus' life; each has its own translation. Be that as it may, the Gospel of John presents the life of Jesus from an alternate perspective, and seeks to show over all the incredible importance for the world and the believer.

John the Elder, most likely born into the world

a Jew, was one who had a profound Christian experience, and thought long upon a mind-blowing significance of Christ's life. Maybe he was a Christian preacher - a "prophet" he would have been called in the first century-and had frequently spoken on the topics he finally treated in his works.

He wrote so as to check mistakes into which a few Christians of his day had fallen, and to present a positive assessment of Jesus Christ in wording that would be comprehended by Hellenistic readers. His works have a style and vocabulary of their own, and present a few great ideas over and over.

John thought of life and the world as far as great contrasts: light and darkness, goodt and evil, truth and error, life and death, God and the world. He didn't think so much of the complexities between "this age" and "the age to come," the same number of other New Testament writers did, as between the temporal order and the eternal order.

Huge numbers of these complexities help us to remember the thoughts introduced by the Essences in the Dead Sea Scrolls. They don't establish an exhaustive and certifiable "dualism,"

Dr. John Thomas Wylie

for John accepted that God made this world and is in charge of it; his last victory over darkness and evil is assured. The present age is under the impermanent control of Satan, "the ruler of this world" (12:31; 14:30; 16:11), but Christ has defeated him and made possible his destruction in the life of the believer (12:31; I John 3:8).

John presents Jesus most importantly as the revealer of God. In his compositions we discover three of the extraordinary confirmations about God: "God is spirit" (4:24 RSV); "God is light" (I John 1:5 RSV); and "God is love: (I John 4:8, 16 RSV). God is frequently called Father by Jesus, and he may become Father to the believer.

In the Gospel of John, Jesus is an eternal divine being who existed with God from the beginning, who came to earth and lived among men as an human being in the flesh, was crucified, and returned to heaven, but would return (evidently in spiritual form) to be with his own and receive them to himself.

In this Gospel, Jesus carries on with his life on earth calmly with an incredible confidence. He completely knows the end from the beginning. In addition to the fact, not only does he knows God completely, but he knows all men (2:25).

Jesus reveals God in his whole life and in his person. "No one has ever seen God; the only Son, who is in the bosom of the Father, he has made him known" (1:18). "I and the Father are one" (10:30). "He who has seen me has seen the Father," he says to Philip (14:9). For John the whole of the ministry of Jesus is significant; he doesn't put a similar great emphasis on the crucifixion and resurrection that Paul does. In his Gospel, the torturous killing (crucifixion) is the glorification of Jesus; in the majority of the remainder of the New Testament, the glorification comes after the crucifixion.

The message of the Gospel of John is presented clearly in the opening words:

In the beginning was the Word, and the Word was with God, and the Word was God. He was in the beginning with God; all things were made through him, and without him was nothing made that was made. In him was life, and the life was the light of men...And the Word became flesh and dwelt among us, full of grace and truth; we beheld his glory, glory as of the only Son from the Father (1:1-4, 14).

Here the English "Word" translates the Greek word logos, which it can render only defectively (imperfectly). As the logos, Jesus is the "utterance" of God, however he is also the agent of God in creation, and the mediator between man and God. After the opening sentences, the Gospel doesn't use this word in this sense, but the presentation of the life of Jesus concurs with the opening sentences, and they serve to set the life of the human Jesus against the background of time eternity.

John uses for Jesus practically all the titles that are found in other parts of the New Testament. He is teacher, rabbi, prophet, the Messiah (left untranslated in 1:41; 4:25), the Christ, Lord, the Lamb of God, Savior of the world, Son of man (used essentially of the heavenly being, not to underscore his humanity), the King, and Son of God, Jesus knows the Father perfectly, is at one with him, and reveals him to man.

The peak of the Gospel is reached in the confession of Thomas when he sees the risen Lord and cries out: "my Lord and my God!" (20:28). This is one of few verses in the New Testament in which Jesus is called God.

One of the characteristic highlights of the Gospel of John is that in it Jesus habitually speaks of himself. John presents Jesus as saying seven extraordinary "I AMs": I am the bread of life; he who comes to me shall not hunger, and he who believes in me shall never thirst" (6:35). "I am the light of the world; he who follows me won't walk in darkness, but will have the light of life" (John 8:12 RSV). "I am the door of the sheep" (John 10:7 RSV). "I am the good shepherd. The good shepherd lays down his life for the sheep" (John 10:11). "I am the resurrection and the life; he who believes in me, though he die, yet shall he live, and whosoever lives and believes in me shall never die" (John 11:25, 26). "I am the way, and the truth, and the life; no one comes to the Father, but by me" (John 14:6). "I am the true vine, and my Father is the vinedresser" (John 5:1).

In these statements we can see a lot of what John thought concerning the person of Jesus, and what believing in him would accomplish for the disciples.

In the writings of John "faith" happens only a once: "This is the triumph that overcomes the world, our faith" (I John 5:4 KJV). However he as often as possible uses the action verb "believe," and calls upon man to believe. The purpose for the Gospel is expressed along these lines: "These (words) are written that you may believe that Jesus is the Christ, the Son of God, and that believing you may have life in his name": (20:31).

First John 5:1 RSV says, "Every one who believes that Jesus is the Christ is a child of God, and every one who loves the parent loves the child." Belief is, accordingly, in the first instance, a belief about Jesus, that he is the Christ and God's Son. In any case, it is likewise belief in Christ, and self-surrender to him, as Paul had stressed. Belief in Christ leads to union with Christ, which John as a rule calls "abiding in" Christ.

The person who has faith in Christ experiences, as per John, a new birth, or birth "from above." a similar Greek expression can mean either "born again" or birth "from above."

To Nicodemus Jesus says, "Truly, truly, I say to you, unless one is born anew, he can't see the kingdom of God" (3:3). Apart from chapter 3 of the Gospel, being born again, or born of God, shows up much of the time in I John. The new birth is a heavenly change (a supernatural transformation) of man's nature, fundamentally the same as Paul's concept of the Christian's being a new creature in Christ.

While John is concerned for the salvation of the individual, he is likewise intrigued by the formation of the church as the body of the believers. "Church" doesn't show up in the Gospel, however it definitely has in view the church when it speaks of believers in Christ as the flock, of which he is the shepherd (10:16); and the branches, of which Christ is the vine (15:1). Furthermore, the church was likewise in John's psyche when he talked about Jesus' gathering "into one the children of God who are dispersed abroad: (11:52).

One of the momentous or remarkable passages in the Gospel is the area in Jesus' intercessory prayer in which he appeals to God for the solidarity (unity) of his disciples in the course of his life and of the those who believe in him through their word. His prayer is "that they may all be one; even as thou, Father, art in me, and I in thee, that they likewise may be in us, so that the world may believe that thou hast sent me: (17:21). John lived at a time when the solidarity of the church was undermined by disagreements and bogus teachers, as the Epistles show.

To the individuals who have faith in him, Christ gave the promise of the Paraclete. This is one of the interesting expressions of John's compositions, occurring in 14:16, 26; 15:26;

16:7, and I John 2:1. The Greek expression of which Paraclete is a transliteration is rendered in the Gospel by the Revised Standard Version as Counselor, and by the King James Version as Comforter (in the sense of "strengthener"); in I John 2:1 both render it as advocate.

The parakletos was truly "one who was called alongside another: to serve as legal counsel, witness, or the like. He was counselor in this sense, or one's backer under the steady gaze of an appointed authority, before the judge. Twice the Paraclete is known as the Spirit of truth, and once the Holy Spirit. Jesus promises that the Paraclete will go to the disciples after he leaves them, to guide them into all truth, and glorify Jesus by convincing men that unbelief in him is sin (16:7-14).

In I John 2:1 the "advocate" with the Father is "Jesus Christ the righteous." Somewhat these passages are hard to harmonize. In any case, we should take note of that in the first mention of the Paraclete, the promise is of "another Paraclete." This recommends Jesus himself on earth is a counselor and advocate of men.

There are signs in the Gospel that Jesus expected to come back to earth as spirit, with the goal that he is the Paraclete. First John, composed long after the lifetime of Jesus, would thus be able to write of Jesus himself as the Paraclete.

The gift of God to those who believe in Jesus is eternal life. This is one of the most characteristic phrases of John, and he uses it in a special way. Some of the time the single word "life" signifies the same thing.

The one of a kind element of John's perspective on "eternal life" is that he believes it to be a present possession of the believer. "Truly, truly, I say to you, he who hears my word and believes him who sent me, has eternal life; he does not come into judgment, but has passed from death to life" (5:24). "Truly, truly, I say to you, he who believes has eternal life" (6:47). There are numerous such passages in John's writings.

Judgment, in like manner, is something which is as of now already present in the lifetime of Jesus.

He who believes in him is not condemned; he who does not believe is condemned already, because he has not believed in the name of the only Son of God. And, this is the judgment, that the light has come into the world, and men loved darkness rather than light, because their deeds were evil (3:18, 19).

However, there are passages which talk about future judgment and of the future coming of Christ. "Try not to wonder about this; for the hour is coming, when all who are in the tombs will hear his voice and come forth, those who have done good, to the resurrection of life, and those who have done evil, to the resurrection of judgment" (5:28, 29).

Jesus at times discusses his coming back to earth: "When I go and prepare a place for you, I will come again and will take you to myself, that where I am you may be also" (14:3).

At times it is clear, in any case, that the coming of Christ is a coming of the spiritual Christ to the believer, as in 14:23: "If a man loves me, he will keep my word, and my Father will love him, and we will come to him and make our home with him."

Interpreters of John have experienced issues in reconciling the two sets of ideas. Is eternal life a present or a future possession? Is judgment present or future? A few scholars believe that passages, for example, 5:28, 29 which discuss future judgment are additions to John's own writing.

Others believe that the author has not made his very own view joining perspective on eternal life with the traditional Christian hopes for the future. Maybe there is a trace of validity in the last mentioned, but the contrasts between the two are not so great.

For John "eternal life" isn't so much everlasting status (immorality) or life that is perpetual, as it is a new quality of life. One who is born from above has infused into his life a new being. Eternal life is like life "in Christ" in Paul's works, a mystical-ethical union with Christ.

However it is an actual life whose consummation and full realization lie in the future, rather than in the current life of this world. The ideas show up together, with an implied moral admonishment (exhortation), in I John 3:2, 3 RSV: "Beloved, we are God's children now; it doesn't yet appear what we shall be, but we know that when he appears we shall be like him, for we shall see him as he is. What's more, and every one who therefore hopes in him purifies himself as he is pure."

John gives this definition of eternal life in John 17:3 RSV: "This is eternal life, that they know thee the only true God, and Jesus Christ whom thou hast sent." To know God is to know that he is one and to know his true nature as uncovered (revealed) in Jesus Christ; to know Jesus Christ is to have faith in him and accept his revelation. Eternal life is similar to the kingdom of God, a phrase used in 3:3, 5. Nicodemus is informed that he can't enter the kingdom unless he is born of water and the Spirit (born anew).

Everlasting life (Eternal life) acknowledgment of God's sovereignty so that one is reconciled to him; it implies that one has gone from death to life, and escape the power of death to destroy him; it brings him the ability to obey God and bear much fruit. When one has eternal life, he is in Christ and Christ in him.

First John obviously expresses that one who is born of God has escaped from sin's power, and is capable of living a sinless and perfect life: "No one born of God commits sin; for God's nature (or seed) abides in him, and he can't sin because he is born of God" (I John 3:9; see also 3:6; 5:18 and cf. John 8:31-47).

However, there is a reasonable, realistic note in I John 5:16, 17, in which the reader is bidden to appeal (pray) to God for a brother who has committed a transgression (sin) that is not mortal.

Love is one of the catchphrases in John's

writings, found again and again in the Gospel and I John. It was out of love for the world that God gave his only Son, to bring to every believer eternal life (3:16).

The life of Jesus was a real life dependent on love for God and love of man; "having loved his own who were in the world, he loved them to the end" (13:1). The life of the Christian is a life of love toward God and Christ and toward his fellow men. Over and over the Christian is informed that to obey God means to love his brethren. The absolute most grounded and most significant words are in I John:

Beloved, let us love one another; for love is of God, and he who loves' is born of God and knows God. He who does not love does not know God; for God is love... We love, because he first loved us. If any one says, "I love God," and hates his brother, he is a liar; for he who does not love his brother whom he has seen, can not love God whom he has not seen... For this is the love for God, that we keep his commandments (4:7-8, 19-20; 5:3).

# Chapter Five

## Unity In Diversity

THE THREE CREATIVE FIGURES of the New Testament are Jesus, Paul, and John. Since we have talked about their message, and the earliest Christian preaching, we have secured the fundamentals of the New Testament message. For the rest of the books, the reader should refer consul the Bible and study the rest of the books of the New Testament. They present scarcely present any new ideas, and some were concerned about neutralizing bogus or false teachings.

The New Testament all in all shows a rich diversity in its message. To some extent this is to be attributed to paradox, or even inconsistency. A great part of the richness is the result of improvement over the course of the spread of the Christian faith from its small beginnings in Palestine.

Is there a unity within this diversity? There is, and it is to be found in the person and life of Jesus Christ, and his meaning for the individuals who believe in him. At the danger of distortion (oversimplification), we may sum up the unifying of the New Testament message as follows:

(1) Jesus' birth to the world and earthy vocation were purposed by God for the saving of humanity. This is communicated in two different ways: Jesus fulfilled the Old Testament prophecies; and he was a pre-existing divine being, present with God even at the creation. Along these lines Jesus was not a man who became divine; nor was he a good man who was deified by his followers. He was the manifestation (incarnation) of God, and a true revelation of the divine nature.

(2) In his earthly vocation Jesus lived as a real man. He lived in the flesh, being totally human, enticed as other men were but without sin. The New Testament dismissed as bogus (rejected as false) all teaching that Jesus just "seemed" to exist as a human being. Note that Jesus came as 100% God and 100% man (in this manner, the God-man).

(3) While the whole of Jesus' earthlyl life was significant, the torturous killing (crucifixion) and resurrection were of central importance. The story of these events solidified (crystalized) early; they

occupied almost a exclusive place in the theology of Paul.

Their significance was clarified in a variety of ways, however in any event the torturous killing (crucifixion) exhibited man's absolute insidiousness, for it implied the cruel, unfeeling homicide of an innocent man; it uncovered God's grace and mercy; and it demonstrated Christ's complete obedience to God and his love for his fellow men.

The resurrection of Jesus implied that he had conquered death, and that the Christ in whom men believed was a living, risen Lord.

(4) Throughout the New Testament is found the "hope" of Christ's return in glory and judgment. This was from the outset distinctive, and controlled numerous aspects of the life of the church. As the return was delayed, the hope turned out to be less energetic, however was not deserted nor abandoned.

John's Gospel offered an option in contrast to desire for the visible, material return of Christ with its emphasis on eternal life as a present possession and the coming to Christ in spirit into the lives of believers.

All through the New Testament, the hope of Christ's return is one of the bases of the intrigue for purity of life, and preparedness to receive him at whatever point he may come.

(5) The New Testament message has a variety of ways for communicating the manner in which the believer appropriates for himself the benefits of Christ's life, death, and resurrection. Jesus summoned men to repent, follow him, and be prepared for the kingdom of God.

Paul stresses faith as the doorway to man's becoming a new creature "in Christ." John called for belief that Jesus is the Christ, in order that one may be born again and received eternal life. There is an essential solidarity (basic unity) in these three unique ways for putting the Christian message, in spite of the various terms they employ.

(6) The New Testament message called men to life in the Christian church. Regardless of whether Jesus explicitly proposed to establish a church, he called men to follow him as his disciples, and from them he chose a select group of apostles.

After the resurrection, the Christian people community was a party within Judaism, recognized by the way that it believed the

Messiah had already come. Over the span of time the church isolated itself totally from Judaism, and became organized. It was viewed as the true Israel, the body of Christ, God's own people, the community of the new covenant.

(7) The New Testament message consistently demanded a high expectation of ethical quality (morality). It couldn't relinquish its foundations in Judaism, and didn't wish to do as such. Among Gentiles the Christian message of freedom in Christ was at times misconstrued as permitting license and even rebellion (lawlessness).

Against such misunderstanding Paul and others endeavored overwhelmingly. The ethical standards of the New Testament are to a great extent equivalent to those of the Old Testament. There is a wonderful understanding that love is the fulfilment of God's command, so man's moral obligation might be summed up in the Old Testament directive (Leviticus 19:18). "You shall love your neighbor as yourself" (Matthew 22:39; Romans 13:9; James 2:8; I John 3:11).

Concerning the dynamic of the moral life, Jesus was convinced that "every sound tree bears good fruit" (Matthew 7:17). Paul taught that the man who is a new creature "in Christ" will show in his life the fruit of the Spirit (Galatians 5:22). John said that he who is born anew (or from above) abides in Christ, and Christ abides in him, so that he obeys in light of the fact that he loves.

# Bibliography

The Apostolic Preaching And Its Developments (1944), (new edition) London, Eng.: Hodder & Stoughton, LTD

Morton, E. S. (1929) The Place Of Morality In The Thought Of Paul. Chester, PA.: (Publisher UNK)

Primitive Christianity In Its Contemporary Setting (1956) New York, NY.: Living Age Books, Meridan Books

The Ethics Of Paul (1957) Nashville, TN.: Abingdon Press, Apex Books.

The Holy Bible (1964) Authorized King James Version. Chicago, Ill.: J. G. Ferguson

The Holy Bible (1982) New International Version. Grand Rapids, MI.: Thomas Nelson (Used By Permission)

The Holy Bible (1978) New York, NY.: New York International Bible Society (Used By Permission)

The Holy Bible (1953) The Revised Standard Version. Nashville, TN.: Thomas Nelson & Sons (Used By Permission)

The Holy Bible (1901) The American Standard Version. Nashville, TN.: Thomas Nelson (Used By Permission)

The Holy Bible (1959) The Berkeley Version. Grand Rapids, MI.: Zondervan (Used By Permission)

The Holy Bible (1977) The New American Standard Bible. USA.: The Lockman Foundation (Used By Permission)

The Holy Bible (1996) The New Living Translation. Wheaton, Ill.: Tyndale House Publishers (Used By Permission)

The New Testament In The Language Of The People (1937, 1949) Chicago, Ill.: Charles B. Williams, Bruce Humphries, Inc, The Moody Bible Institute (Used By Permission)

The New Testament In Modern English (1958) New York, NY.: J. B. Phillips, Macmillan (Used By Permission)

The Wycliff Bible Commentary (1962, 1968) Nashville, TN.: Chicago, Ill.: The Southwestern Company, The Moody Bible Institute Of Chicago

# About The Author

THE REVEREND DR. JOHN Thomas Wylie is one who has dedicated his life to the work of God's Service, the service of others; and being a powerful witness for the Gospel of Our Lord and Savior Jesus Christ. Dr. Wylie was called into the Gospel Ministry June 1979, whereby in that same year he entered The American Baptist College of the American Baptist Theological Seminary, Nashville, Tennessee.

As a young Seminarian, he read every book available to him that would help him better his understanding of God as well as God's plan of Salvation and the Christian Faith. He made a commitment as a promising student that he would inspire others as God inspires him. He understood early in his ministry that we live in times where people question not only who God is; but whether miracles are real, whether or not man can make a change, and who the enemy is or if the enemy truly exists.

Dr. Wylie carried out his commitment to God, which has been one of excellence which led to his earning his Bachelors of Arts in Bible/Theology/ Pastoral Studies. Faithful and obedient to the call of God, he continued to matriculate in his studies earning his Masters of Ministry from Emmanuel Bible College, Nashville, Tennessee & Emmanuel Bible College, Rossville, Georgia. Still, inspired to please the Lord and do that which is well – pleasing in the Lord's sight, Dr. Wylie recently on March 2006, completed his Masters of Education degree with a concentration in Instructional Technology earned at The American Intercontinental University, Holloman Estates, Illinois. Dr. Wylie also previous to this, earned his Education Specialist Degree from Jones International University, Centennial, Colorado and his Doctorate of Theology from The Holy Trinity College and Seminary, St. Petersburg, Florida.

Dr. Wylie has served in the capacity of pastor at two congregations in Middle Tennessee and Southern Tennessee, as well as served as an Evangelistic Preacher, Teacher, Chaplain, Christian Educator, and finally a published author, writer of many great inspirational Christian Publications such as his first publication:

***"Only One God: Who Is He?" – published August 2002 via formally 1ˢᵗ books library***

*(which is now AuthorHouse Book Publishers located in Bloomington, Indiana & Milton Keynes, United Kingdom)* which caught the attention of **The Atlanta Journal Constitution Newspaper.**

Dr. Wylie is happily married to Angel G. Wylie, a retired Dekalb Elementary School teacher who loves to work with the very young children and who always encourages her husband to move forward in the Name of Jesus Christ. They have Four children, 11 grand-children and one great-grandson all of whom they are very proud. Both Dr. Wylie and Angela Wylie serve as members of the Salem Baptist Church, located in Lilburn, Georgia, where the Reverend Dr. Richard B. Haynes is Senior pastor.

Dr. Wylie has stated of his wife: "she knows the charm and beauty of sincerity, goodness, and purity through Jesus Christ. Yes, she is a Christian and realizes the true meaning of loveliness as the reflection as her life of holy living gives new meaning, hope, and purpose to that of her husband, her children, others may say of her, "Behold the handmaiden of the Lord." A Servant of Jesus Christ!

# About The Book

THE TITLE PAGE OF the second part of the Christian Bible reads: The New Testament, ordinarily called "The New Covenant." The New Testament Or "New Covenant" is the story of the appearance on earth of Jesus Christ to be the mediator of a new covenant, and of his followers who made up the people of the new covenant.

When Jesus gave his disciples the cup at the Last Supper, he stated: "This cup is the new covenant (new agreement) in my blood" (I Corinthians 11:25; cf. Mark 14:24). Paul believed himself to be the clergyman of a new covenant (II Corinthians 3:6), and Hebrews sees the fulfilment of Jeremiah's prophecy of a new covenant (Jeremiah 31:31-34) in the covenant of which Jesus was the mediator (8:8-13; 10:16-18).

In review the Old Testament, the concept of a covenant is key to the comprehension of the Old Testament. It is likewise central to the New Testament, notwithstanding the way that the word itself happens rarely. The new covenant is the fulfilment of the old, bringing to realization it promises, and not a sharp break from it. The concept of covenant ties together, as opposed to separating the Old and New Testaments.

Dr. John Thomas Wylie

Printed in the United States
By Bookmasters